No Nonsense English

6-7 years

GW00420424

Contents

www.bond11plus.co.uk

Handwriting practice

Practise the joined up letters. Go over the grey letters first. Make sure you start at the dot and follow the arrows. Do not lift your pencil when writing the joined letters. Then copy the joins a few times in the spaces.

in	ut	ve
ve	ok	sh
es	ri	oa
ee	ea	ow
ky	ha	od
er	ai	oy
re	fu	ru
ot	aw	al
ol	ow	ng

oc   ke   fl

wh   ie   ly

ly   ap   ck

ie   ly   ap

ck   if   he

ft   wr   ff

ew   th   ac

dig   cat   log

ill   sat   ear

More practice? Go to www

ow

The letters **ow** are in lots of words.

cl**ow**n

cow

1. Read the words in the box. Choose a word to finish each sentence.

cow	crown	down	growls	clown

a My dog _ _ _ _ _ _ _ .

b A king wears a _ _ _ _ _ _ .

c We get milk from a _ _ _ .

d The people laughed at the _ _ _ _ _ _ .

e The boy fell _ _ _ _ the stairs.

2. Put the rhyming words in the right list.

bow	growl	town
frown	howl	now
how	down	fowl

cow

clown

owl

_____   _____   _____

_____   _____   _____

_____   _____   _____

How did I do?

Total 8

More practice? Go to www

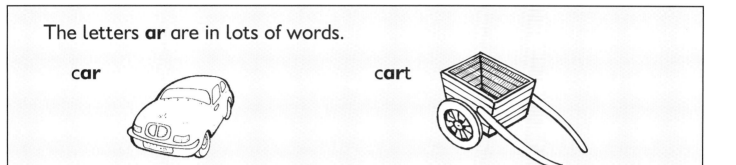

The letters **ar** are in lots of words.

car   **cart**

1.   Read the words in the box. Choose a word to finish each sentence.

jar	star	park	barks	card

a My dog _ _ _ _ _ .

b Jam comes in a _ _ _ .

c I like playing in the _ _ _ _ .

d I have made a birthday _ _ _ _ .

e The Sun is a _ _ _ _ .

2.   Put the rhyming words in the right list.

part	ark	far
dark	dart	bark
bar	jar	tart

park   cart   car

_____   _____   _____

_____   _____   _____

_____   _____   _____

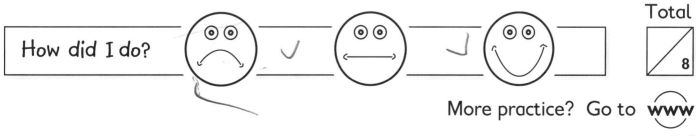

How did I do?   Total

More practice? Go to www

5

oo

In some words **oo** can make a short **uh** sound.

h**oo**d

h**oo**k

1. **Sort the rhyming words.**

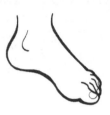

look	stood	soot
good	took	foot

ook

_____

_____

ood

_____

_____

oot

_____

_____

2. **Think of an oo word to match these clues.**

   a You read this. _____

   b You do this to food to make it ready to eat. _____

   c A big black bird like a crow. _____

   d A small river. _____

   e You knit scarves or jumpers with this. _____

3. **Write a sentence with as many oo words in it as you can.**

_____

_____

How did I do?

Total

/9

More practice? Go to www

oy and oi

The letters **oy** and **oi** are in lots of words. They make the same sound.

coin

toys

1. **Write oy or oi to spell these words correctly. Say the words you have made.**

    a p _ _ n t

    b c _ _ l

    c j _ _

    d j _ _ n

    e b _ _

    f f _ _ l

    g s _ _ l

    h e n j _ _

2. **Use one oy word and one oi word in sentences of your own.**

    a _____

    _____

    b _____

    _____

How did I do?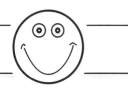

Total

/10

More practice? Go to www

Vowels and consonants

The alphabet is made up of **vowels** and **consonants**.

There are **five vowels**: a e i o u

and **21 consonants**: b c d f g h j k l m n p q r s t v w x y z

1. **Circle the letters that do not belong in these groups.**

a vowels:

   i c u a o s e

b consonants:

   b m e x t a w

c vowels:

   z o a n i v u

d consonants:

   h f n o r j i

2. **Write the missing vowels to make these words.**

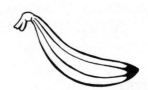  

a b _ n _ n _   **b** p _ n c _ l   **c** _ n _ m _ l s

3. **Write the missing consonants to make these words.**

 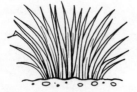

a _ u _ _   **b** _ e a _ _ e _   **c** _ _ a _ _

How did I do?

Total
/10

More practice? Go to

8

Long vowel sounds

The letters **ee**, **ai**, **ie**, **oa** and **oo** make long sounds in words.
The sounds can be made with different groups of letters.
Say each row of words. Listen for the common sound.

ee	f**ee**t	s**ea**t		
ai	tr**ai**n	n**a**m**e**	pl**ay**	
ie	l**ie**	b**i**t**e**	h**igh**	fl**y**
oa	b**oa**t	p**o**l**e**	sh**ow**	
oo	m**oo**n	t**u**n**e**	fl**ew**	bl**ue**

1. **Join the words with the same long vowel sound. Add a word to each pair. The first one has been done for you.**

   a speak   pie   _____

   b true   main   _____

   c goat   spoon   _____

   d stay   blow   _____

   e cry   meet   <u>treat</u>_____

2. **Replace the long vowel sound in these words with a different long vowel sound to make new words.**

   a mean   _____

   b groan   _____

   c tooth   _____

   d feed   _____

   e cane   _____

   f stale   _____

How did I do?

Total

/10

More practice? Go to

air, are, ear and ere

> Some letter patterns sound the same but have different spellings.
>
> I can see a ba**re** b**ear** over th**ere** by the ch**air**.

1. **Put the words with the same spellings in the right list.**

| hare   hair | stair   stare | fair   fare | pair   pear | there   where |

are   air   ear   ere

_____   _____   _____   _____

_____   _____   _____

_____

                 _____

2. **Choose a word from the box to match each picture.**

| scare   bear   square   tear   stare   mare |

a

_____

b

_____

c

_____

d

_____

e

_____

f

_____

Total

How did I do?   😞   😐   😊   /10

More practice?   Go to   www

Words that mean more than one of something are called **plurals**.

   boat boat**s**   apple apple**s**

We add **s** to lots of words when we write plurals.

1. **Do these sentences make sense? Mark them with a ✓ or a X.**

   a There are lots of plum on the tree. ___

   b I wrote a poems at school today. ___

   c I went swimming with my three friends. ___

   d I gave my mum a birthday cards. ___

2. **Write these sentences out again, changing the highlighted words so that they mean more than one. The first one has been started for you.**

   a My mum bought **a banana** at the supermarket.

   My mum bought six _____

   b I played in the park with **a friend**.

   _____

   c My birthday cake had **a candle** on it.

   _____

   d I have read **a book** this week.

   _____

How did I do?   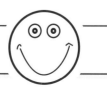   Total

8

More practice? Go to www

Doing words – ing

> Doing words ending in **ing** can tell us what is happening now.
>
> I am read**ing** a book.
> We are look**ing** at some pictures.

1. **Add ing to the words to finish the sentences. Read the finished sentences.**

a We are go_____ to the seaside.

b She is play_____ outside.

c The dog is jump_____ over the wall.

d Tom is push_____ his bicycle.

e Mum is look_____ for me.

QUICK TIP!
Remember!
Drop the **e**.
Add **ing**.

2. **Add ing to these words.**

a ride _____   b have _____

c like _____   d love _____

e come _____   f give _____

3. **Use these ing words in sentences of your own.**

a calling _____

_____

b helping _____

_____

c making _____

_____

Total

How did I do?

 14

More practice? Go to www

Doing words – ed

'I jump'

Doing words tell us:
- **what** is done
- **when** it is done.

We usually add **ed** to a doing word to show that something happened in the past.

'I jump**ed**'

1. Write these in the past.

a We laugh. _____

b You play. _____

c They walk. _____

d I paint. _____

QUICK TIP!
Find the doing word. Add **ed**.

2. Write these in the past.

a I smile at Mum. _____

b We wave to our friend. _____

c They like apples. _____

d You save stamps. _____

e We move house. _____

3. Write a sentence with an ed doing word of your own.

_____

_____

QUICK TIP!
Remember: If it ends in **e**, just add **d**!

How did I do?

Total

10

More practice? Go to www

Sentences 1

Sentences must:
- begin with a **capital letter**
- end with a **full stop** or **question mark**
- make **sense**.

What is that dog's name?
His name is Jack**.**

1. **Join these to make sentences. The first one has been done for you.**

a Can I go   your bicycle?

b The old lady lives   are going to school.

c Do you like riding   out to play?

d The boys and girls   in that little house.

2. **Make these into sentences.**

a This old dog _____

b What is _____

c The people came _____

d My dad helps _____

e Will you _____

QUICK TIP!
Do you need a
full stop or a
question mark?

3. **Write a sentence about what you like doing.**

_____

_____

4. **Write a sentence about what you don't like doing.**

_____

_____

How did I do?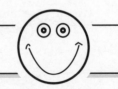

Total
/10

More practice? Go to

Capital letters

Special naming words have capital letters.
Places are special naming words.

River **D**ee   **L**eeds   **M**ount **E**verest

1. Your address will have lots of special naming words. Write your address.

_____

_____

_____

_____

2. Underline the special naming words in these sentences.

a Our town is called Haywards Heath.

b There are lots of boats on the River Dart.

c I live in Park Street.

3. Write these special naming words with capital letters.

a green street

b hilltown

_____   _____

c river hull

d mount tor

_____   _____

How did I do?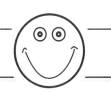

Total
8

More practice? Go to

Exclamation marks

Sentences end in an **exclamation mark** when something unusual or exciting happens.

The house is on fire!

Help!

1. **Add a full stop, question mark or exclamation mark to finish these sentences.**

   a   We played with the dog__

   b   What are you doing__

   c   The tree is going to fall__

   d   Can you see that bird__

   e   I am frightened__

   Try writing a few exclamation marks.

   !

2. **Write what you think the people in the pictures are shouting. Use exclamation marks to end the sentences.**

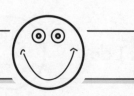

_____   _____

_____   _____

How did I do?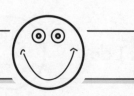

Total

7

More practice? Go to www

16

Linking words

Some words are useful for linking sentences. They can help to show the order in which things happen and make the text easier to read.

These are some linking words. They can go at the beginning or in the middle of sentences.

after   **meanwhile**   **during**   **before**   **then**

1. **Underline the linking words in these sentences.**

   a   Samir put his bucket and spade in the car then went to find his swimming trunks.

   b   Meanwhile, his sister was still looking for her swimming costume!

   c   Before lunch, Samir and his sister built sandcastles.

   d   After lunch they went for a swim in the sea.

2. **Write five sentences about what you have done today. Think about the order in which you did things. Use some linking words in your sentences.**

   (5 marks)

   _____

   _____

   _____

   _____

   _____

   _____

How did I do?

Total

q

More practice? Go to www

Stories with familiar settings

This story is set in a house and its garden.

What other stories have you read that are in a similar setting?

This is the beginning of a story called *David's Dinner*.

David lived in an old country cottage. It had a thatched roof and a yellow door. And its walls were covered in honeysuckle.

In a corner of the cottage garden was a vegetable patch and behind that was a field with a big oak tree. A cow lived in the field.

One morning David's mother asked him to go to the vegetable patch and get a lettuce and some carrots for dinner. She gave him a crust of warm, fresh bread to take with him.

After he had picked as many vegetables as he could carry, David thought he would go into the field to say hello to the cow. So he put the lettuce and carrots down in a big heap on the grass, and he put his crust of bread on top of them. Then he climbed over the fence.

By John Kershaw

1. **What colour was the door?**

   The door was _____

2. **What did David's mum ask him to get from the garden?**

   She asked him to get a _____ and some _____

3. **What did his mum give David to take with him?**

   She gave him _____

4. **Write about where you live.**

   _____

   _____

How did I do?

Total

4

More practice? Go to www

Poems with familiar settings

Poets sometimes write about places that are familiar to us. The poet who wrote this doesn't tell us where his poem is set but you can work it out from what he says!

Monday Morning
Moaning, groaning,
mumbling, grumbling,
glowering, showering,
rubbing, scrubbing,
washing, sploshing,
groping, soaping,
howling, towelling,
splashing, dashing,
muttering, buttering,
crunching, munching,
sighing, tying,
brushing, rushing,
cramming, slamming,
and off to
school.
      John C. Head

1. **In the poem, what do you think the poet is ....**

   a rubbing? _____

   b washing? _____

   c buttering? _____

   d brushing? _____

2. **Think about what you do in the morning before going to school.
   Write your own ing words.**   *(6 marks)*

   _____   _____   _____

   _____   _____   _____

How did I do?   😟   😐   😊

Total
/10

Instructions

Instructions tell us how to do something or how to make something.

Read the instructions and answer the questions.

How to make chocolate icing

 1. Put some icing sugar into a bowl.

 2. Add some chocolate powder.

 3. Hold the bowl under a dripping tap.

 4. Mix with a spoon as the water drips into the bowl.

1. **What are the instructions for?** _____

2. **How many instructions are there?** _____

3. **Do you think they are easy to follow?** _____

4. **What other sorts of instructions can you think of?** _____

_____

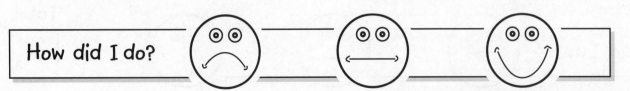

Total

How did I do?

4

More practice? Go to

Diagrams and labels

Instructions can be easier to understand when there are labelled diagrams to go with them.

QUICK TIP!
Write clear labels with arrows pointing to parts of the pictures.

Draw and label a diagram for each of these instructions.

Making a sandcastle

1.

Dig some sand and fill the bucket with it.

2.

Pat the sand down so that it is level with the top of the bucket.

3.

Turn the bucket upside down and lift it up off the sandcastle.

4.

Decorate your sandcastle!

How did I do?

Total

4

More practice? Go to www

1. **Write these words. Look for ow, ar and oo.**

a

b

c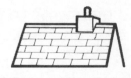

d

    _ _ _   _ _ _ _   _ _ _ _   _ _ _ _ _

2. **a** Write the vowels in the alphabet.

    _____

   b Write the consonants in the alphabet.

    _____

3. **Complete the sentences using these long vowel sound words.**

     feet   n**a**m**e**   b**oa**t   fl**y**

   a I wish I could _____ .

   b I have ticklish _____ .

   c What is your _____ ?

   d I have never been on a _____ .

4. **Write these words. Look for air or are.**

a

b

c

    _ _ _ _ _   _ _ _ _ _   _ _ _ _ _

5. Make these words plural.

a   biscuit   _____

b   bubble   _____

c   computer   _____

d   curtain   _____

6. Add ing and ed to each of these words. Look out for the words which end in e!

(4 marks, $\frac{1}{2}$ mark for each)

	ing	**ed**
a pull	_____	_____
b smile	_____	_____
c push	_____	_____
d kick	_____	_____

7. Find the special naming words. Write them with capital letters.

town	england	mary	bank	london	frog	freddy

_____   _____

_____   _____

8. Finish these sentences with a full stop, a question mark or an exclamation mark.

a   What did you say____

b   John walked to school____

c   They have missed the bus____

9. Underline the linking word in these sentences.

a   I had my lunch then went out to play.

b   I am allowed to have pudding after I've eaten my dinner.

c   I went out to play while my mum dressed my baby sister.

Total

☐ /31

More practice?   Go to   www

ch

The letters **ch** are in lots of words.
They can come at the beginning of words.

chair

chimp

They can come at the end of words.

bun**ch**

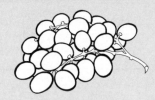

cat**ch**

1. **Add ch to complete these words.**

    a pin _____

    b _____ ip

    c lun _____

    d _____ in

    e flin _____

    f _____ ick

2. **Join the rhyming words. Add another rhyming word to each pair.**
    The first one has been done for you.   *(4 marks, ¹/₂ mark for each)*

    a hutch   match   _____

    b munch   itch   _____

    c hatch   lunch   _____

    d ditch   sketch   _____

    e fetch   much   touch _____

How did I do?

Total 10

More practice? Go to

ph

When you find the letters **ph** together in a word they make the sound **f**.

tele**ph**one

1. **Use the ph words in the box to finish these sentences.**

> telephone   photograph   elephant   Christopher   photocopier

a

She is using the

— — — — — — — — — .

b

She is using the

— — — — — — — — — — — .

c

This is an

— — — — — — — .

d

My name is

— — — — — — — — — — — .

e

She is taking a _ _ _ _ _ _ _ _ _ _ .

What do you notice about this word?

— — — — — — — — — — — — — — — —

— — — — — — — — — — — — — — — —

How did I do?

Total

6

More practice? Go to www

wh

Many question words begin with **wh**.
> **What** are you doing?
> **Where** are you going?
> **When** did you see her?
> **Why** are you sad?

QUICK TIP!
Watch out for **who**.
It sounds different
but it is a **wh**
question word.

1. **Write a question beginning with each of these wh question words.**

a When _____

b What _____

c Where _____

d Why _____

e Who _____

2. **Here are some more wh words. Can you match each word to a picture?**

a

_____

b

_____

| wheel |
| whale |
| whistle |
| whisper |

c

_____

d

_____

How did I do?

Total

q

More practice? Go to

The letters **er** are at the end of lots of words.

broth**er**   sist**er**

Look at the picture clues. Fill in the er crossword.

Across

1

4

7

8

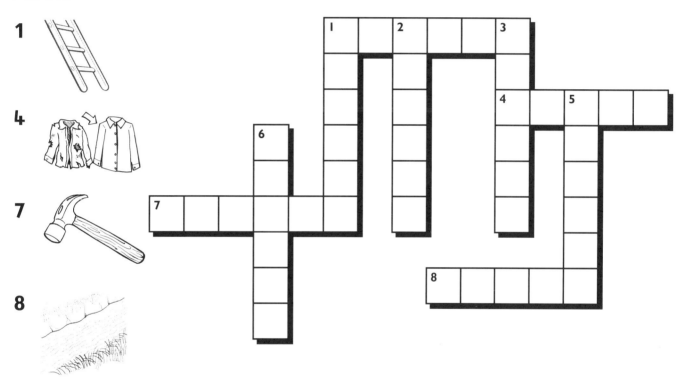

Down

1   2   3   5   6

How did I do?   Total

More practice? Go to www

er, ir and ur

The letters **er**, **ir** and **ur** can make the same sound in words.

fern  bird  church

1. **Read the words in the box. Choose a word from the box to finish each sentence.**

girl	curl	fern	first	burst

a A _ _ _ _ is a plant.

b Abdul came _ _ _ _ _ in the race.

c She is a _ _ _ _ .

d The balloon _ _ _ _ _ .

e There is a _ _ _ _ in her hair.

2. **Write three ir and ur words of your own:**

ir   ur

_____   _____

_____   _____

_____   _____

3. **Write a sentence using some of your ir and ur words.**

_____

_____

How did I do?

Total

12

More practice? Go to

or, oor, aw, au and ore

Say these words.

stor**m**   **p**oor   **str**aw   **P**aul   **m**ore

They all contain the same sound but the sound is spelt differently.

1. Complete the sentences using the words from the box.

torch	dawn	core	daughter	door

a   I like apples but not the apple _____ .

b   That girl is my _____ .

c   The Sun rises at _____ .

d   I have a key to the _____ .

e   I use a _____ to help me see in the dark.

**2. Write the answers to these clues.
The answers will have or, oor, aw, au or ore in them.**

a   You stand on this in a room.   — — — — — —

b   A cat's foot.   — — —

c   A summer month.   — — — — — — —

d   You use this to eat your dinner.   — — — — —

e   You do this if you are tired.   — — — —

f   You do this if you get a goal.   — — — — — —

QUICK TIP!
Remember capital
letters for special
naming words!

How did I do?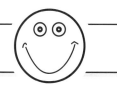

Total

11

More practice? Go to www

Compound words

Compound words are made by joining together two smaller words.

snow   +   man   =   snowman

1. **Join these words together.**

   a book + case   = _____

   b tea   + pot   = _____

   c day   + light = _____

   d under + ground = _____

2. **Write the words and then join them together.**

   a

   _____ + _____ = _____

   b

   _____ + _____ = _____

   c

   _____ + _____ = _____

How did I do?

Total

7

More practice? Go to

Syllables 1

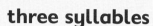

Syllables are parts of words.
Some words have only **one syllable**:

dog

Some words have more than one syllable:

two syllables	**three syllables**
sis ter = sister	an o ther = another
Mon day = Monday	fam i ly = family

1. **Write your first name.** _____

How many syllables does your name have? _____

2. **Put these words in the correct list.**   *(9 marks)*

out	brother	pushing
December	shouted	girl
remember	way	Saturday

one syllable   two syllables   three syllables

_____   _____   _____

_____   _____   _____

_____   _____   _____

3. **Write your own words with ...**

a one syllable.   _____

b two syllables.   _____

c three syllables.   _____

How did I do?				Total 13

More practice? Go to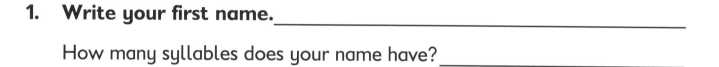

Opposites

Lots of words have **opposites**.

big

little

Opposites are also known as **antonyms**.
Some antonyms are the same word with letters added to the front.

pack

unpack

1. **Match each word with its opposite.**

a	day	up
b	undress	untie
c	down	true
d	tie	dress
e	untrue	night
f	big	front
g	after	unwell
h	under	little
i	well	before
j	back	over

How did I do?

Total
10

More practice? Go to

32

No Nonsense
English

6-7
years

Parents' notes

What your child will learn from this book

Bond No Nonsense will help your child to understand and become more confident at English. This book features the main English objectives covered by your child's class teacher during the school year. It provides clear, straightforward teaching and learning of the essentials in a rigorous, step-by-step way.

This book begins with some **handwriting practice**. Encourage your child to complete this carefully and to continue writing neatly throughout the book.

The three types of lessons provided are:
Letters and words – these cover the alphabet, phonics and spelling.
Sentences – these cover punctuation and grammar.
Shared reading – these cover reading stories/poems and short comprehension questions.

The shared reading pages have been designed for you to read with your child. You could read the text to your child, encourage him/her to read to you or join in as you read.

How you can help

Following a few simple guidelines will ensure that your child gets the best from this book:

- Explain that the book will help your child become confident in their English work.
- If your child has difficulty reading the text on the page or understanding a question, do provide help.
- Encourage your child to complete all the exercises in a lesson. You can mark the work using this answer section (which you will also find on the website). Your child can record their own impressions of the work using the 'How did I do' feature.

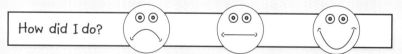

- The 'How am I doing?' sections provide a further review of progress.

Using the website – www.bondlearning.co.uk

- The website provides extra practice of every skill in the book. So if your child does not feel confident about a lesson, they can go to the website and have another go.
- For every page of this book you will find further practice questions and their answers available to download.
- To access the extra practice pages:
  1. Go to www.bondlearning.co.uk
  2. Click on 'English'
  3. Click on '6–7 Years'
  4. Click on the lesson you want.

Bond No Nonsense 6–7 years Answers

① ow p4
1 **a** growls **b** crown **c** cow **d** clown **e** down
2 bow   town   growl
   now   frown   howl
   how   down   fowl

② ar p5
1 **a** barks **b** jar **c** park **d** card **e** star
2 ark   part   bar
   dark   tart   far
   bark   dart   jar

③ oo p6
1 look   stood   soot
   took   good   foot
2 **a** book **b** cook **c** rook **d** brook **e** wool
3 Answers will vary

④ oy and oi p7
1 **a** point **b** coil **c** joy **d** join **e** boy
   f foil   **g** soil **h** enjoy
2 Answers will vary

⑤ Vowels and consonants p8
1 **a** i ⓒ u a o Ⓢ e
   b b m ⓔ x t ⓐ w
   c Ⓩ o a ⓝ i Ⓥ u
   d h f n ⓞ r j ⓘ
2 **a** banana **b** pencil **c** animals
3 **a** duck   **b** feather **c** grass

⑥ Long vowel sounds p9
1 **b** spoon **c** blow **d** main **e** pie
2 **a** moon, main or moan
   b grain or green
   c teeth
   d food
   e cone
   f stole

⑦ air, are, ear and ere p10
1 hare   hair   pear   there
   stare   stair   where
   fare   fair
           pair
2 **a** tear **b** stare **c** scare **d** mare **e** bear
   f square

⑧ Plural – add s p11
1 **a** ✗ **b** ✗ **c** ✓ **d** ✗
2 **a** My mum bought six bananas at the supermarket.
   b I played in the park with two friends. (number may vary)
   c My birthday cake had seven candles on it. (number may vary)
   d I have read three books this week. (number may vary)

⑨ Doing words – ing p12
1 **a** going **b** playing **c** jumping **d** pushing **e** looking
2 **a** riding **b** having   **c** liking   **d** loving   **e** coming
   f giving
3 Answers will vary

⑩ Doing words – ed p13
1 **a** We laughed.   **b** You played.
   c They walked.   **d** I painted.
2 **a** I smiled at Mum.   **b** We waved to our friend.
   c They liked apples. **d** You saved stamps.
   e We moved house.
3 Answers will vary

⑪ Sentences 1 p14
1 **b** The old lady lives in that little house.
   c Do you like riding your bicycle?
   d The boys and girls are going to school.

2 Answers will vary
3 Answers will vary
4 Answers will vary

⑫ Capital letters p15
1 Answers will vary
2 **a** Our town is called Haywards Heath.
   b There are lots of boats on the River Dart.
   c I live in Park Street.
3 **a** Green Street   **b** Hilltown
   c River Hull   **d** Mount Tor

⑬ Exclamation marks p16
1 **a** We played with the dog.
   b What are you doing?
   c The tree is going to fall!
   d Can you see that bird?
   e I am frightened!
2 Answers will vary

⑭ Linking words p17
1 **a** then **b** Meanwhile **c** Before **d** After
2 Answers will vary

⑮ Stories with familiar settings p18
1 yellow
2 lettuce / carrots
3 a crust of warm, fresh bread
4 Answers will vary

⑯ Poems with familiar settings p19
1 Answers will vary but may include
   a arms **b** face **c** toast **d** teeth
2 Answers will vary

⑰ Instructions p20
1 How to make chocolate icing.
2 There are four instructions.
3 Answers will vary
4 Answers will vary

⑱ Diagrams and labels p21
Answers will vary but pictures should represent the text next to them.

How am I doing? p22
1 **a** owl **b** moon **c** roof **d** shark
2 **a** a e i o u
   b b c d f g h j k l m n p q r s t v w x y z
3 **a** I wish I could fly.
   b I have ticklish feet.
   c What is your name?
   d I have never been on a boat.
4 **a** hare   **b** stairs   **c** fair
5 **a** biscuits **b** bubbles **c** computers **d** curtains
6 **a** pulling pulled
   b smiling smiled
   c pushing pushed
   d kicking kicked
7 England Mary London Freddy
8 **a** What did you say?
   b John walked to school.
   c They have missed the bus!
9 **a** then **b** after **c** while

⑲ ch p24
1 **a** pinch **b** chip **c** lunch **d** chin **e** flinch
   f chick
2 **b** lunch **c** match **d** itch **e** sketch

20 ph p25

1 **a** She is using the telephone.
   b She is using the photocopier.
   c This is an elephant.
   d My name is Christopher.
   e She is taking a photograph.
      It begins and ends with ph.

21 wh p26

1 Answers will vary
2 **a** wheel   **b** whisper   **c** whale   **d** whistle

22 er p27

Across	Down
1 ladder	**1** letter
4 newer	**2** dinner
7 hammer	**3** runner
8 river	**5** winner
	6 summer

23 er, ir and ur p28

1 **a** A fern is a plant.
   b Abdul came first in the race.
   c She is a girl.
   d The balloon burst.
   e There is a curl in her hair.
2 Answers will vary
3 Answers will vary

24 or, oor, aw, au and ore p29

1 **a** core   **b** daughter   **c** dawn   **d** door   **e** torch
2 **a** floor   **b** paw   **c** August   **d** fork   **e** yawn
   F score

25 Compound words p30

1 **a** bookcase   **b** teapot   **c** daylight   **d** underground
2 **a** buttercup   **b** staircase   **c** lighthouse

26 Syllables 1 p31

1 Answers will vary
2

one syllable	two syllables	three syllables
out	brother	December
way	pushing	remember
girl	shouted	Saturday

3 Answers will vary

27 Opposites p32

1 **a** day   night
   b undress   dress
   c down   up
   d tie   untie
   e untrue   true
   f big   little
   g after   before
   h under   over
   i well   unwell
   j back   front

28 Doing words – past tense 1 p33

1 **b** went   **c** came   **d** got   **e** did   **f** made
2 **a** He took a bun.
   b He dug the garden.
   c She wrote a letter.

29 Commas p34

1 **a** We have a cat, a dog, a hamster and a goldfish.
   b On Monday, Tuesday and Wednesday I ride my bicycle.
   c We have PE on Monday, Wednesday and Thursday.
2 Answers will vary

30 Speech bubbles p35

1 Answers will vary

31 Speech marks p36

1 **a** "Is your name Sam?" asked the teacher.
   b "This is my brother," said Helen.
   c "It is time to go!" shouted Dad.
   d Mum said, "You can go out to play."
2 **a** The boy called, "I am over here!"
   b "That tree has fallen over," said Tom.
   c "It took us a long time," moaned Sally.
   d Mr Timms said, "That is very good".
3 "When are we playing the match?" asked Harry.
   John replied, "On Monday after school."

32 Does it make sense? 1 p37

1 **a** ✓   **b** ✗   **c** ✓   **d** ✗   **e** ✓
2 **a** I am excited about my birthday.
   b They are going to the park after school.
   c She is very happy today.
   d We are having sausages for dinner.

33 Dictionaries p38

1 **b** tree – it has a trunk, branches and leaves
   c house – where people live
   d cat – small furry animal
   e door – something that can be opened and shut
   f jump – to spring up
2 bed   cat   door   house   jump   tree

34 Traditional stories 1 p39

1 Answers will vary

35 Traditional stories 2 p40

1 **a** Hare thought he could run faster than Tortoise.
   b Hare was sure he would win the race.
   c Hare fell asleep under a tree.
   d Tortoise won the race.
2 to   or   is
3 **a** ran   **b** won   **c** awake

36 Indexes p41

1 football   13
   netball   7
   swimming   9
   tennis   3
2 Answers will vary

How am I doing? p42

1 **a** cherry   **b** whisk   **c** photo
2 **a** skirt   **b** herd   **c** burst
3 **a** foot + ball = football
   b rain + coat = raincoat
4 Answers will vary
5 **a** right   **b** low   **c** fast   **d** dirty   **e** soft
   f near   **g** happy
6 **a** I made cakes.
   b I ran fast.
   c I drank orange juice.
7 **a** I can run faster than my mum, my dad and my sister.
   b Ying, Billy, Tom and I play football together.
8 **a** "Where are we going today?" asked Luma.
   b The teacher shouted, "No running in the classroom!"
9 **a** They are playing in the park.
   b We are watching cartoons.

37 ea p44

1 peach   thread
   each   dread
   cream   spread
   sea   weather
   feast   tread
   neat   heavy
2 Answers will vary

38 Syllables 2 p45

1 **b** often   **c** forest   **d** golden   **e** asleep
   f woman   **g** landed
2 **a** an + i + mals
   b hosp + pi + tal
   c news + pa + per

39 Word endings – ful p46

1 **a** careful   **b** dreadful   **c** hopeful   **d** helpful
   e wonderful   **f** painful   **g** useful   **h** thoughtful
2 Possible answers include:
   a Terry saw a Cheéful boy..
   b Tamu saw a colourful rainbow.
   c Yosef has a handful of sand.
3 **a** pitiful   **b** merciful   **c** dutiful   **d** bountiful

40 Word endings – ly p47

1 **a** He rode his bike <u>quickly</u>.
   b The dog yelped <u>noisily</u>.
   c The wind blew <u>strongly</u>.
   d She wrote <u>neatly</u> in her book.
2 Answers will vary but could include:
   a loudly   **b** quietly   **c** beautifully
   d slowly   **e** scarily

41 Doing words – past tense 2 p48

1 **a** I saw a bird in the tree.
   b They made a mess.
   c We came here by bike.
   d I walked to the park.
2 Answers will vary.

42 Synonyms p49

1
drink	noise	hat
sip	sound	hood
gulp	blare	cap
swallow	din	helmet

2 **a** cried   **b** yelled   **c** shouted   **d** asked

43 Gender words p50

1 **a** father   **b** daughter
   c grandmother   **d** son
   e grandfather   **f** mother
2 **a** sister   **b** uncle
   c princess   **d** husband

44 Describing words p51

1 Answers will vary
2 Answers will vary
3 Answers will vary

45 Same spelling, different sound p52

1 **a** minute   **b** lead   **c** close   **d** wind
   e minute   **f** wind   **g** close   **h** Lead

46 Spelling irregular words p53

1 Check your child's spelling of the words.

47 Statements and questions p54

1 **a** Is he going to the shops?
   b Is your name Gary?
   c Is that a crab?
2 Answers will vary

48 Does it make sense? 2 p55

1 **a** ✗   **b** ✓   **c** ✓   **d** ✗   **e** ✓
2 **a** She was wearing her best dress.
   b I was enjoying playing football.
   c They were washing the car.
   d The children were looking forward to their holiday.

49 Narration p56

Answers will vary but should contain similar information to these.
1 He got out of bed.
2 He brushed his teeth.
3 He got dressed.
4 He had his breakfast.

50 Sentences 2 p57

1 **a** Sentences must begin with a capital letter.
   b Sentences must end with a full stop, question mark or exclamation mark.
   c Sentences must make sense.
2 **a** My Aunt Ella always brings cakes when she visits us on Tuesdays.
   b When I am older I want to play football with Samir on Saturdays.
   c How do I get to Canterbury from here?
   d Help, I am frightened of the dark!

51 Rhyming poetry p58

1 **a** all   **b** day   **c** spoon   **d** Jill   **e** add

52 Humorous poetry p59

1 **a** instead
   b been
2 When the upside down man goes to bed his feet are on the pillow instead of his head.
3 The back to front man can't tell where he is going because he is facing the wrong way.

53 Writing about books p60

1 Answers will vary

54 Information books p61

1
Insects have	Spiders have
three body parts	two body parts
six legs	eight legs

2 A baby spider can grow a new leg. An adult spider cannot grow a new leg.

How am I doing? p62

1 **a** Boats sail on the sea.
   b The bags were full of shopping and very heavy.
2 **a** window   **b** pencil   **c** ruler
3 **a** wishful   **b** powerful   **c** pitiful
4 **a** smoothly
   b silently
   c friendly
5 **a** I was making / I made dinner with my mum.
   b We were playing / We played a game.
6 Answers will vary but could include:
   a beautiful, lovely, attractive
   b miserable, unhappy
   c hot
   d slim, lean, skinny, slender
7
male	female
dad	girl
man	sister
nephew	actress

8 Answers will vary
9 close
10 Is she drying her hair?
11 We were going to the cinema to watch a film.

Doing words – past tense 1

When we are writing about things that have already happened we put the doing word in the **past tense**.

Usually we add **ed** to the doing word.

He brush**ed** his hair.

Some doing words do not follow the rule.

She **caught** the ball.

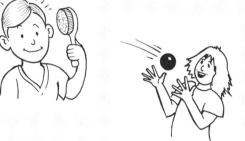

1. **Match the now doing words with the yesterday doing words. The first one is done for you.**

now		yesterday
a	say	came
b	go	did
c	come	said
d	get	made
e	do	went
f	make	got

> QUICK TIP!
> **Now** words are called the **present tense**. They are happening **now**. **Yesterday** words are called the **past tense**. They have already happened.

2. **Finish the sentences. Use the words in the box.** | dug   wrote   took |

a

b

c

He _____ a bun.

He _____ the garden.

She _____ a letter.

How did I do?

Total 8

More practice? Go to www

33

Commas

We use a **comma** to **separate** the items in a list.

Mum**,** Dad**,** my sister and I went out.

The last two items are joined by **and**.

I like apples, pears, bananas **and** oranges.

1. Copy these sentences. Add the missing commas.

a We have a cat a dog a hamster and a goldfish.

_____

b On Monday Tuesday and Wednesday I ride my bicycle.

_____

c We have PE on Monday Wednesday and Thursday.

_____

2. Use these lists in sentences of your own.

a red   green   blue   yellow

_____

_____

b milk   water   tea   sugar

_____

_____

Total

How did I do?

/ 5

More practice? Go to

Speech bubbles

When we write the words people say we can use **speech bubbles**.

We call writing the words which people say **direct speech**.

1. **What do you think they are saying? Fill in the speech bubbles.**

How did I do?

Total

4

More practice? Go to www

Speech marks

If we write direct speech in stories we have to use **speech marks** and say who is speaking. We put speech marks at the **beginning** and **end** of the spoken words.

"Is that your dog?" asked Sumey.

"No. I have never seen it before," said Molly.

1.   Underline the spoken words.

a   "Is your name Sam?" asked the teacher.

b   "This is my brother," said Helen.

c   "It is time to go!" shouted Dad.

d   Mum said, "You can go out to play."

> **QUICK TIP!**
> You don't always have to use **said** when you say who is speaking.

2.   Put speech marks around the spoken words.

a   The boy called, I am over here!

b   That tree has fallen over, said Tom.

c   It took us a long time, moaned Sally.

d   Mr Timms said, That is very good.

> Practice writing some speech marks here.
>
> "   "

3.   Write the words from the speech bubbles using speech marks.   (2 marks)

_____ asked Harry.

John replied, _____

How did I do?

Total

10

More practice? Go to

36

When writing a sentence it is important that the parts of the sentence agree with each other.

I am going swimming. ✓   **I are** going swimming. ✗

We am going swimming. ✗   **We are** going swimming. ✓

These parts of sentences agree with each other:

I am   you are   she is   he is   they are   we are

1. Do these sentences make sense? Mark them with a ✔ or a ✗.

a   She is my sister. _____

b   I is riding my bicycle. _____

c   They are in the swimming pool. _____

d   He are my brother. _____

e   He is reading a book. _____

2. Write these sentences correctly.

a   I is excited about my birthday.

_____

b   They am going to the park after school.

_____

c   She are very happy today.

_____

d   We is having sausages for dinner.

_____

How did I do?   Total

More practice? Go to www

Dictionaries

A **dictionary** tells us:
- the meaning of words
- how to spell words.

A dictionary is arranged in alphabetical order.

1. Match the word to its meaning.

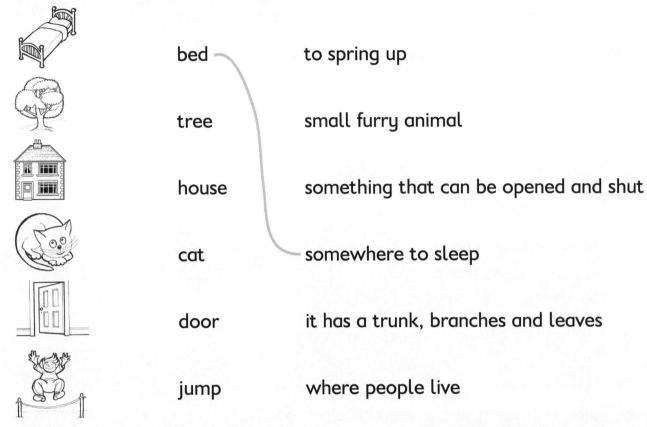

bed	to spring up
tree	small furry animal
house	something that can be opened and shut
cat	somewhere to sleep
door	it has a trunk, branches and leaves
jump	where people live

2. Now put the words in the order you would find them in a dictionary.

(6 marks)

QUICK TIP!
Look at the first letter of each word and remember your alphabet.
a b c d e ...

How did I do?

Total

11

More practice? Go to www

Traditional stories 1

The Hare and the Tortoise is a **traditional story**. Lots of adults will know the story because they heard it when they were children.

The Hare and the Tortoise

1. Hare thought he was good at running. Hare told Tortoise he could run faster than him.

2. Tortoise said they should have a race. Hare thought this was very funny. He said he would win the race.

3. Hare and Tortoise began the race. Hare ran much faster than Tortoise and was soon a long way ahead.

4. Hare was sure he would win the race, so he sat down for a little rest.

---

1. **What do you think might happen? Write how you think the story ends.**

_____

_____

_____

_____

The story is continued in the next lesson…

   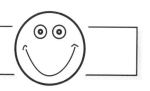

Traditional stories 2

Perhaps you already know the ending to the story about the hare and the tortoise.

If you haven't heard the story before did you guess the ending correctly? Read on to find out!

5. Tortoise just kept plodding on. He passed Hare asleep under a tree.

6. By the time Hare was awake, Tortoise had won the race.

1. Finish the sentences.

a Hare thought he could run _____ than Tortoise.

b Hare was sure he would _____ the race.

c Hare fell _____ under a tree.

d Tortoise _____ the race.

2. Find three different two-letter words in tortoise.

__ __   __ __   __ __

3. What is...

a the past tense of **run**?   __ __ __ __

b the past tense of **win**?   __ __ __

c the opposite of **asleep**?   __ __ __ __ __ __

How did I do?

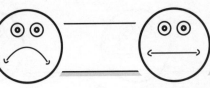

Total

10

More practice? Go to

Indexes

We find an **index** at the back of an information book.

An **index** tells us where to find things in the book.

An index is set out in **alphabetical order**.

	page
bears	7
cats	2
dogs	14
elephants	4
frogs	10

1. You could find these things in a book about sport. Use them to make an index. *(4 marks)*

QUICK TIP!
Look at the
first letter of
each word.

football   13

tennis   3

swimming   9

netball   7

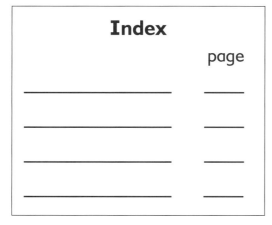

Index

page

_____   _____

_____   _____

_____   _____

_____   _____

2. Why do you think an index is useful?

_____

_____

How did I do?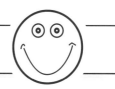

Total

/5

More practice? Go to

How am I doing?

1. Write these words. Look for ch, ph or wh.

a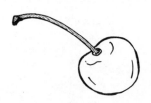

_ _ _ _ _ _

b

_ _ _ _ _

c

_ _ _ _ _

2. Write these words. Look for er, ir or ur.

a

_ _ _ _ _

b

_ _ _ _ _

c

_ _ _ _ _

3. Write these compound words.

a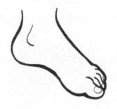

_____ + _____ = _____

b

_____ + _____ = _____

4. Write a word with ...

a one syllable. _____

b two syllables. _____

c three syllables. _____

5. Match the opposites.

a   left   near

b   high   dirty

c   slow   happy

d   clean   low

e   hard   right

f   far   fast

g   sad   soft

6. Write these sentences in the past tense.

a   I make cakes.   _____

b   I run fast.   _____

c   I drink orange juice. _____

7. Add the missing commas to these sentences.

a   I can run faster than my mum my dad and my sister.

b   Ying Billy Tom and I play football together.

8. Add the missing speech marks to these sentences.

a   Where are we going today? asked Luma.

b   The teacher shouted, No running in the classroom!

9. Write these sentences correctly.

a   They is playing in the park.   _____

b   We am watching cartoons.   _____

Total

27

More practice? Go to www

ea

We find **ea** in lots of words. Sometimes it sounds like the **e** in b**e**d.

h**ea**d   br**ea**d

Sometimes it sounds like the **e** in m**e**.

eat   b**ea**k

1. **Say these words. Put them in the right columns for their sounds.**

each	dread	cream	spread	sea
weather	feast	tread	neat	heavy

peach   thread   *(10 marks)*

_____   _____

_____   _____

_____   _____

_____   _____

_____   _____

2. **Use one word from each list in a sentence of your own.**

a _____

_____

b _____

_____

How did I do?

Total

12

More practice? Go to **www**

44

Syllables 2

Syllables are parts of words.
Splitting a word into its syllables helps with spelling.

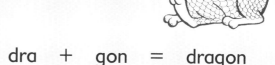

morn + ing = morning   dra + gon = dragon

---

1. **Join these syllables to make new words. The first one has been done for you.**

a	gar	est	_garden_
b	of	ed	_____
c	for	den	_____
d	gold	ten	_____
e	a	man	_____
f	wo	sleep	_____
g	land	en	_____

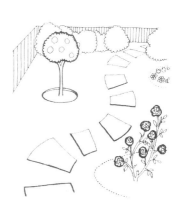

2. **Look at the pictures. Write the three-syllable words.**

   a    _ _ + _ + _ _ _ _ = _____

   b    _ _ _ + _ _ + _ _ _ = _____

   c   _ _ _ _ + _ _ + _ _ _ = _____

How did I do?      Total

More practice? Go to www

Word endings – ful

The letters **ful** are often added to a word when we want to say what something is like.

This is a beauti**ful** rose.

When we put **ful** at the end of a word it has only one **l**.

1. Add ful to these words. Read the words.

a care _____

b dread _____

c hope _____

d help _____

e wonder _____

f pain _____

g use _____

h thought _____

2. Think of a ful word to finish these sentences.

a Terry is a _____ boy.

b Tamu saw a _____ rainbow.

c Yosef has a _____ of sand.

If you want to add **ful** to a word ending in **y** you have to change the **y** to **i** first.

plent**y**   plent**i**ful

3. Add ful to these words.

a pity _____

b mercy _____

c duty _____

d bounty _____

How did I do?

Total ⬚/15

More practice? Go to

Word endings – ly

The letters **ly** are added to some words to show **how** things are done.

She sang.

loud
quiet

She sang loud**ly**.

loud**ly**
quiet**ly**

1. **Read these sentences. Underline the words which tell you how something was done.**

a He rode his bike quickly.

b The dog yelped noisily.

c The wind blew strongly.

d She wrote neatly in her book.

2. **How could these things be done? Use a different ly word to finish each sentence.**

a The lion roared _____ .

b The mouse squeaked _____.

c The bird sang _____ .

d The cow walked _____ .

e The snake hissed _____ .

How did I do?   Total
9

More practice? Go to www

Doing words – past tense 2

We add **ed** to lots of doing words to make the **past tense**.

jump – jump**ed**   play – play**ed**

Some doing words have different past tenses.

catch – **caught**   run – **ran**

1. **Write these sentences again putting the doing words in the past tense.**

   a I see a bird in the tree.

   _____

   b They make a mess.

   _____

   c We come here by bike.

   _____

   d I walk to the park.

   _____

QUICK TIP!
Ask yourself what you would write if the event happened yesterday.

2. **Use these past tense doing words in sentences of your own.**

   a found _____

   _____

   b laughed _____

   _____

How did I do?

Total

6

More practice? Go to

Synonyms

Some words mean the **same** or **nearly the same** as each other. These words are called **synonyms**.

big
large
huge

small
little
tiny

1. **Put the words in the box in the right list.**

(9 marks)

sip	hood	gulp	sound	cap
blare	helmet	swallow	din	

words which
mean **drink**

words which
mean **noise**

words which
mean **hat**

_____

_____

_____

_____

_____

_____

_____

_____

_____

2. **All of these words mean the same, or nearly the same, as said. The letters have got muddled up. Your challenge is to sort them out! You have been given the first letter of each word.**

a r d c e i

c _____

b l y e l e d

y _____

c h t s d e u o

s _____

d d a k s e

a _____

How did I do?   _____

Total

/13

More practice? Go to www

49

Gender words

We use **gender words** to say whether a person or animal is male or female.

Boy is a
male word.

Girl is a
female word.

1. **Use the gender words in the box to label the members of this family.**

| mother | grandmother | son | father | daughter | grandfather |

a _____

b _____

c _____

d _____

e _____

f  _____

2. **Fill in the missing gender words.**

	male		**female**
a	brother	→	_____
b	_____	←	aunt
c	prince	→	_____
d	_____	←	wife

How did I do?

Total
10

More practice? Go to www

Describing words

Using **describing words** makes your writing more interesting and gives extra information.

My dad makes cakes.
My **wonderful** dad makes **tasty** cakes.

QUICK TIP!
Remember, colours are describing words.

1. **Add describing words to these sentences to make them more interesting. Look at the pictures to help you decide what words to add.**

a The _____ cake was covered in _____ icing.

b The _____ dog liked his _____ bone.

2. **Choose two describing words and put a comma in between them.**

a The rabbit was dreaming about a _____ carrot.

b It was a _____ day.

3. **Write a sentence about your favourite hobby. Use some describing words to make it more interesting.**

_____

_____

How did I do?

Total
5

More practice? Go to www

Same spelling, different sound

Sometimes words that are spelt the same can sound different.

Say these sentences and listen to the different sounds.

She cried and a **tear** ran down her face.

There was a **tear** in the piece of paper.

1. **Complete the sentences using these words. Each word will be used twice but will mean two different things. Say the sentences.**

close	lead	wind	minute

a One _____ is the same as 60 seconds.

b I put my dog on his _____ and took him for a walk.

c He stood very _____ to me.

d My dad has to _____ up the clock to make it work.

e Tiny means small but _____ means something is even smaller.

f I don't like it when the _____ blows.

g He said the shop would _____ at five o'clock.

h _____ is a type of metal.

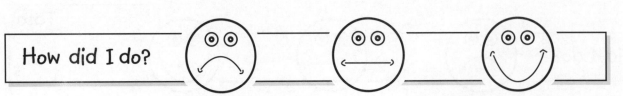

How did I do?

Total

8

More practice? Go to

Spelling irregular words Letters and words

Some words don't follow a pattern to help you spell them – they just have to be learned!

When you are learning to spell new words try this method:

1 **Look** at the word.
2 **Cover** the word.
3 **Write** the word.
4 **Check** your spelling.

1. **Look, cover, write and check these words one at a time.**

Look and cover	write	check
above	*above*	✓
world		
Earth		
asked		
does		
often		
during		
friends		
great		
any		
whole		

How did I do?

Total
10

More practice? Go to www

Statements and questions

Some sentences **tell** us things.

It is raining today.

Some sentences **ask** us things.

Is it raining today?
When did it rain?

We can make telling sentences into asking sentences.

1. **Make these telling sentences into asking sentences.**

a He is going to the shops.

_____

b My name is Gary.

_____

c That is a crab.

_____

QUICK TIP!
Remember your
question marks.

2. **Write a telling sentence and an asking sentence about the picture.**

_____

_____

_____

_____

 How did I do?

Total

5

More practice? Go to

54

Does it make sense? 2

When writing a sentence it is important that the parts of the sentence **agree** with each other.

If something has already happened (in the past) then these words agree with each other.

I was   you were   she was   he was   they were   we were

1. **Do these sentences make sense? Mark them with a ✔ or a ✕.**

a He were the winner. ____

b They were very happy. ____

c I was very sleepy. ____

d We was on our way to the shops when I hurt my foot. ____

e She was helping her brother with his homework. ____

2. **Write these sentences correctly.**

a She were wearing her best dress.

_____

b I were enjoying playing football.

_____

c They was washing the car.

_____

d The children was looking forward to their holiday.

_____

How did I do?

Total
 9

More practice? Go to www

Narration

To **narrate** means you tell the story of something. Narration is often written as if something has **already happened**. This means writing in the **past tense**.

The people **watched** the clown. ✓ (already happened)
The people are **watching** the clown. ✗ (happening now)

1. **Narrate the story that is being told in these pictures. Remember, tell the events as if they have already happened.**

Getting ready for school

1.

_____

_____

_____

2.

_____

_____

_____

3.

_____

_____

_____

4.

_____

_____

_____

How did I do?

Total

4

More practice? Go to

Sentences 2

Writing clear **sentences** is very important. They help people to understand what you are trying to say.

1. **Complete these sentences to show how much you know about writing clear sentences!**

   a Sentences must begin with a c_____ l_____ .

   b Sentences must end with a f_____ s_____ ,

   q_____ m_____

   or e_____ m_____ .

   c Sentences must make s_____ .

   > QUICK TIP!
   > Remember that special naming words must begin with a **capital letter**.

2. **Write these sentences correctly.**

   a my aunt ella always brings cakes when she visits us on tuesdays

   _____

   _____

   b when i am older i want to play football with samir on saturdays

   _____

   c how do i get to canterbury from here

   _____

   d help, i am frightened of the dark

   _____

How did I do?   Total

More practice? Go to www

57

Rhyming poetry

Poems sometimes rhyme.

Where are the rhyming words in this poem?

Nursery Rhymes

I've many nursery rhymes to tell.
There's Humpty and his wall,
Little Jack Sprat and young Tom Thumb,
I expect you've heard them all.

Remember poor Miss Muffet, who
Was eating her curds and whey?
A spider came to pay a call –
And really spoilt her day!

And what about the jumping cow
Who leapt over the moon,
Leaving behind a fiddle and a cat
And a dish running off with a spoon?

Let's not forget the boy and the girl
Who climbed up that big hill
To fetch some water in a pail.
Yes, that was Jack and Jill.

So many nursery rhymes to tell,
Some happy, funny, sad –
They're not all here, I'm sure of that.
So what others can you add?

QUICK TIP!
Share this poem
with someone
older than you.

1. **Find the rhyming words in the poem.**

    a wall rhymes with __ __ __   **b whey** rhymes with __ __ __

    c moon rhymes with __ __ __ __ __   **d hill** rhymes with __ __ __ __ __

    e sad rhymes with __ __ __

How did I do?

Total
5

More practice? Go to

Humorous poetry

This poem makes people laugh. The title suggests that it is probably a **humorous poem**.

Two Funny Men
I know a man
Who's upside down,
And when he goes to bed
His head's not on the pillow, No!
His **feet** are there instead.

I know a man
Who's back to front,
The strangest man **I've** seen.
He can't tell where he's going
But he knows where he has been.

Spike Milligan

1. **Find the rhyming words.**

   a **bed** rhymes with _____

   b **seen** rhymes with _____

2. **What happens when the upside down man goes to bed?**

   _____

   _____

3. **Why can't the back to front man tell where he's going?**

   _____

   _____

How did I do?

Total
4

More practice? Go to www

Writing about books

> It is a good idea to write down what you think about the books you read.
>
> You need to:
> • record the title and author
> • write what you thought about it.

1. Use this page to write about a book you have just finished reading.

(5 marks)

The book I have just read is called

_____

It was written by

_____

Some of the characters are

_____

_____

The story is about _____

_____

_____

I liked the book because _____

_____

_____

How did I do?

Total
/5

More practice? Go to www

Information books

Information books are sometimes called **non-fiction** books.
Non-fiction books tell us things that are true.

Let's learn about spiders!

Spiders are **not** insects.
A spider has two body parts.
Insects have three body parts.

Spiders mostly have eight legs.
Insects mostly have six legs.

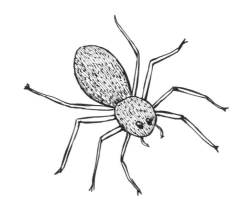

If a baby spider loses a leg, it can grow a new one.
An adult spider cannot grow a new leg.

1. **Finish the chart to show the differences between insects and spiders.**

(4 marks)

Insects have	Spiders have

2. **What can a baby spider do that an adult spider cannot do?**

_____

_____

_____

How did I do?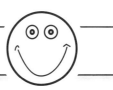

Total [ ] 5

More practice? Go to www

How am I doing?

1. **Complete these sentences with ea words.**

   a Boats sail on the _____ .

   b The bags were full of shopping and very _____ .

2. **Match these syllables to make words.**

   a win   ler

   b pen   dow

   c ru   cil

3. **Add the ending ful to these words.**

   a wish   _____

   b power   _____

   c pity   _____

4. **Add the ending ly to these words.**

   a smooth   _____

   b silent   _____

   c friend   _____

5. **Write these sentences in the past tense.**

   a I am making dinner with my mum.

   _____

   b We are playing a game.

   _____

6. **Write words which mean the same, or nearly the same, as these words.**

   a pretty _____   **b** sad _____

   c warm _____   **d** thin _____

7. **Sort these gender words into male and female columns.**

| girl | dad | man | sister | nephew | actress |

male   **female**

_____   _____

_____   _____

_____   _____

8. **Add describing words to these sentences to make them more interesting.**

   a   There were lots of _____ flowers in the garden.

   b   The _____ lady looked at me and smiled.

9. **Which word that has the same spelling but different sound will complete both of these sentences?**

   a   He asked me to _____ the door behind me.

   b   I stood very _____ to my dad because I was scared.

10. **Make this telling sentence into an asking sentence.**

    She is drying her hair.

    _____

11. **Write this sentence correctly in the past tense.**

    We was going to the cinema to watch a film.

    _____

Total

/24

More practice? Go to www

Try the 7–8 years book

| Lesson 1 | Spelling | ## Long vowel sounds |

Words with **short** vowel sounds usually have one vowel (r**a**t, k**i**t, c**u**b).
Words with **long** vowel sounds can have:

* a **vowel**, then a **consonant** and end in **e** (r**a**t**e**, k**i**t**e**, c**u**b**e**).
* **two vowels** together (b**ai**l, m**oo**d, fr**ui**t, b**ee**, gl**ue**).
* a **vowel** and **y** (h**ay**, b**oy**, th**ey**).

1. **Underline the words with long vowel sounds and circle the words with short vowel sounds.**

   tail   pot   brick   late   sit   sleep   day   cat   away   meat   sow

   set   pie   hat   mite   cute   meet   plate   write   fit   food   lip

2. **Complete these words using ee or ea.**

   a h__ __t   **b** tr__ __   **c** b__ __d   **d** s__ __t   **e** ch__ __se

3. **Write three other words with the same long vowel sound.**

   a soak   _____   _____   _____

   b chew   _____   _____   _____

   c feet   _____   _____   _____

   d train   _____   _____   _____

4. **Fill in the missing long vowel sounds in these sentences.**

   a I cl__ __ned my t__ __th but one of them was l__ __se.

   b Harry pl__ __ed with the brush and spilled p__ __nt on the fl__ __r.

   c The b__ __t in the harb__ __r was qu__t__ rusty and old.

   d The ice cr__ __m was cold and he began to f__ __l c__ __l again.

   e Thr__ __ girls and one b__ __ went d__ __n the sl__d__.

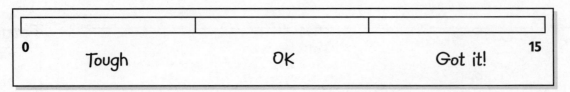

| 0 | | 15 |
| Tough | OK | Got it! |

Total

15

More practice? Go to www

64